HOTHOUSE

Poems by
Karyna McGlynn

Sarabande Books
Louisville, KY | Brooklyn, NY

Library of Congress Cataloging-in-Publication Data

Names: McGlynn, Karyna, author.
Title: Hothouse / Karyna McGlynn.
Description: Louisville, KY : Sarabande Books, [2017]
Identifiers: LCCN 2016049779 | ISBN 9781941411452 (softcover : acid-free
paper)
Subjects: | BISAC: POETRY / American / General.
Classification: LCC PS3613.C486 A6 2017 | DDC 811/.6--dc23
LC record available at https://lccn.loc.gov/2016049779

Cover design by Martin Rock.
Interior and exterior design by Sarabande Books.

Manufacured in Canada.
This book is printed on acid-free paper.
Sarabande Books is a nonprofit literary organization.

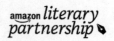

This project is supported in part by an award from the National Endowment for the Arts. The Kentucky Arts
Council, the state arts agency, supports Sarabande Books with state tax dollars and federal funding from the
National Endowment for the Arts.

CONTENTS

Wet Bar

Bath

Basement

Acknowledgments

Even a disagreeable little girl may be lonely, and the big closed house and big bare moor and big bare gardens had made this one feel as if there was no one left in the world but herself.
—Frances Hodgson Burnett, *The Secret Garden*

Oh, we're going to talk about me again, are we? Goody.
—Katharine Hepburn as Tracy Lord in *The Philadelphia Story*

Stay sexy. Don't get murdered.
—*My Favorite Murder* with Karen Kilgariff and Georgia Hardstark

HOTHOUSE

So you want to know where I live?
Come here, love. We'll circle the walls
with my big rococo key & look for a way in.
Say I unlocked the gate, what then?
Bondage porn in a lil' wood trunk? The End?
You say I should become the voyeur,
or at least put a bee through the keyhole.
Instead I traipse around a vacant plot & go
Qui, moi? I *want* to write with the door open
but what to do about it? You might reenter
the room any minute, find me fondling
a dead bee, *naïf* me, inconsolable. Alas,
it still has a sting! But you, so rare,
both reader & lover fused at the stem
of a single hothouse violet hidden
in the very back of my underwear drawer,
purple tongue leaking all over my linens—
Back where my kitsch can't reach,
back in the back where my joy lies,
neither bared nor buried alive.

BEDROOM

and won't, *won't* be naked until this movie is over
because moving images are ultimately greater than—
because sleeping alone is ultimately greater than—
some grunt want whetted and done. And now
I'm crawling across the bed, over the comforter
plashed with huge purple flowers—to you, but not
for you—for my fourteen-year-old self reeking of
controlled heartbreak and watching me do it.
This is why I put on a nightdress and call it
a nightdress, a show. This is the difference
between Karyna and a light bulb: a screw.
Why I make all the ghosts go round and
give your penis the shivers. Because *won't.*
Because *will not* and *will, too.* Because that
little center with the tall fence around itself
can't stick to her script. Lift up your shirt,
I say. Let me smell your armpits, I say. Don't
pretend this is weird. I'm doing it for her,
not you. Shut up, I say. *Let me.* They smell
like pennies, like newsprint, like cumin-stuffed
canaries. Listen to her slow-clapping from her
velvet seat like she's not squiggling down
into the wool of herself. I'll undo your belt
with my teeth, but only this once. I need
to smell your junk, I say. I say we're on
a houseboat. I say we have nothing to wear
but wet sheets, nothing to play with but this
old Scrabble board, missing half the letters.
I'm dying, I say. Open the window.
I'm dying, I say. Bring me all the water.
Go away. I need to dress the set like, *Oops,*
was I wearing these pearls in the shower?
Did I misbutton your button-down when
I threw it on quick like I just heard a crash

in the kitchen? If you loved me you would
see her there in the front row and snap off
the footlights. If you loved me you'd call this
costume a costume. You'd make me pick up
all the seed pearls with my baby teeth.

the whole room fills up with iced tea, something gives:
the sun peels from your window, a sugared lemon,
whole, flaming, hanging there. You tell them they must:
puncture your chest with a straw to suck all the empty
out, but because they say *love* they think they can't hurt
you, even to save your life, which is why you float
up up up, knocking your curled toes and bedeviled
breath hard against the tea-stained ceiling, why you
swim sentry over the oxheart that flooded your bed,
hollowed you out. See it there: big and bobbing wax
fruit, sweating with the effort of its own improbable
being, each burst of wetness a cry to which you are
further beholden, a sweetness trained against your own
best alchemy. Witch, you can only watch this
bloodletting from above, can only amend the deed to
your body: see it say it back, see it like a little rabbit
with a twist on its neck and wish you could *be* that,
being had, being held, but instead you grow wooden and
spin on your back. Propeller? No, there is no getting
away from this, and so: ceiling fan, drowning their
hushed joy, going *schwa schwa schwa* in the bed's
sheath of late afternoon light.

BROKEN BOTTLE OF VANILLA FIELDS

A block away, the football stadium all
      floodlit like the mothership, soaking up
the pitchy dregs of Friday night, calling all
      flying insects home. He kissed me.
There was no heat in it. Only the mouth
      of a small goldfish swallowing
a smaller goldfish. When he touched me
      down there, he expected combustion.
But I was not his dad's red Bronco—idle,
      looping *I smell sex and candy here.*
I was a fat wildflower unstapled
from the pop-up field. I lay very still
and let him strive against me, the grass
      pricking, plasticine. I asked,
Can you hear my heart? I needed
to know it was there. Shh, he breathed.
He looked like a man building his house
      on the slope of some dormant volcano.
Trust me, he said. A drumbeat, and then:
      the drill teams of Travis County gave
a shallow, singular grunt on my behalf,
high-kicking their white sequin cowgirl hats,
lunging forward into the splits.

BIG GAME TROPHY RETURN FANTASY

It's not quite Thanksgiving. Just shy. The uncles stow her
in the hunters' bunkhouse. No place for a girl. From bed,
she gazes at the guns on high racks, the empty beer cans,
Field & Stream, *Hustler*, all the enormous animal heads.
Trophies open & close their glass eyes. A little steam.
The wildebeest & water buffalo step from wood paneling.
Simply, as if from a pond. They shake sawdust
luxuriously from their beards, trampling the guest sheets,
buckling the thin mattress. Her foldout couch retracts
& from this claptrap rises a gamey smell: wet flannel,
old boots, defrosting meat. A girl & her reindeer nightgown
swallowed whole. She falls face-first into dark—borne down
through an underworld of leather & bedsprings.
The lopsided beasts pour forth: bok, boar, kudu, rhino.
They scratch & sniff her future: an opening in the ice,
a truck overturning. This girl thing warming their bodies.
This small hunter neither snuffed nor comforted.
Thanksgiving: an electric flash, the smell of frying venison,
the knife's path along its strop. The deep freeze hums.
They stiffen, backboard ruff around their necks.
Now the screen door opens: it's time to be dead again.

CALIFORNIA KING

Behind closed doors, he bores me.
His frank, functional sensuality
lumbers across the too-big bed
like I am not Goldilocks, like I will
not leap up or eat up his lukewarm
porridge, not clutter up his cutlery.
Now knifing—   Now forking—
His utility ululates me, strains me
of stupid, so what do I care: mouth
full, brain blunted, body a wrung
kneesock on the chairback. *Wait.*
My whole world smells of marinara
& strife. See me spread butter.
See me spread eagle. See me keep
pleasing this rubber Republican dick.
He talks dirty in fleece, but I bleat:
Have some almonds & cream sherry
Oh yes cream sherry! He shushes &
solves for X. Big teddy bear! Eyes like
flat buttons sewn-on & so what?
When I put my finger to his stitches,
he'll spill his Right Stuff on my runway,
touching secondary sex characteristics
like spots on some Twister mat:
right breast yellow, left testicle red,
another flick of the spinner? *Oh sure.*
In his Kingdom of Bore, how richly
he bores me, he bores me, he bores me!

SQUARE ROOMS

Once, we lived in a perfectly square room.
It was drafty but had a working fireplace.

I thought, okay, my life is finally beginning.
He put a big metal chicken in the fireplace.

I loved this. Even though it was very cold
he never told me to put on a sweater.

His ex-wife hated these quirks: his metal
chicken and toy piano, bluebirds nested

in a martini glass, taxidermied squirrel
tableaux, his defacement of Thom Yorke.

Have you ever been in a perfectly square room?
You feel you've arrived at the center of yourself.

On time, for once, everything equidistant and
equally possible. Emily Dickinson's room

was a perfect square, but I didn't get it until
the moment I set foot in his apartment.

I said to myself: okay, I will become his second wife,
his *real* wife, binding and unbinding things, recklessly—

all that symmetry and space, a factory floor!
I will be the New Modern Love Bride!

Wearing a white dress, but warily,
like "okay, I *know*, but fuck, let's *do* this."

A square room can do that to you. But listen:
he had an armoire of leftover wedding champagnes.

One was called "You." One was called "Us."
The most expensive was called "Sex."

We drank them when we ran out of money.
Straight from the bottle, around our perfect

square of a coffee table, in our square room,
making faces at each other in the cold Michigan

sunlight through huge, square windows.
His name was Adam and I thought for sure,

this was it: that we'd go on making things,
naming them, but when we moved South

into rectangular rooms, something stopped.
We sat on opposite ends and drank sparkling wine

from the store. What was it? It didn't have a name.
He kept rearranging little shipwrecks on the shelf.

IN THE FUTURE NO ONE GETS TO CRY

& there will be a hoedown at the polis.
& you & I will go there in our old boots.
& the music will be ho-hum.
& we will hold hands how we do.
& I will have a mouth like a not unhappy hyphen.
& it will never snow.
& you & I will drink only the beer we brought.
& all the chickens will be loosed upon the world.
& we will watch the great wagon wheel turn.
& we will let our charred drumstick cool on the plate.
& the beer will grow warm & why bother.
& the caller will say change partners.
& we will, without protest. ·

LIBRARY

RUSSEL SAYS EVERYBODY IS AUBREY

R & I sit among the minor wreckage of my last relationship
and wonder what to do with it. D only moved to the desert
but it's as if he's dead. Where did he go? What is this stuff?
An alarm clock from the '80s, pair of black patent dress shoes,
sci-fi novel, overcoat covered in cat hair. D is only 27.
Via Skype he tells R: "I feel like my life is finally beginning."
R can't understand this. He feels like his life was over at 24.
Here he is at 34: hot but hopeless, a smart cookie who's just
depressing as shit, sitting there breaking my heart & bumming
me out. We are both the best/worst serial monogamists,
but I don't want to be in this boat with him. He says there's
nothing I can do about it; we're all going down together:
"When's the last time you honestly loved someone?"
"When's the last time you wrote a real goddamn poem?"
"When's the last time you could afford to pay your bills?"
His freshest ex-girlfriend is a 30-year-old stripper who works
at Neiman Marcus. She has an MBA. Her name is Aubrey.
We all hate her. R sighs & picks up D's copy of *Ulysses*.
"I'm starting to think that everybody is Aubrey," he says.
"Everybody is most definitely not Aubrey," I tell him.
"But they are. I'm Aubrey. You're Aubrey. The next person
you fuck is going to be an Aubrey. All that's left is Aubrey."
I cry in the late afternoon sun & say it's just allergies.
R picks up D's books one by one, renaming them Aubrey.

OUR BOOKS, OUR BOOKS

The question is whether to quell this
profligate book writing. Everyone's
"putting out" books. We pulp our words
before pouring them right back in.
How many times can we fold the same bone?

Dad used to fill our slack with dumb conundrums.
He said: Would you rather empty industrial
grease traps for a living or be mute forever?
We said: Mute forever because Our Books, Our Books!
We meant: We will fit Love entirely inside them.

Follow up from Dad: Would you rather write books
for a living or find true love with an oceanographer?
We said: Lichen! Sponges! Immortal Sea Stars!
We meant: Our words will break away and they
will become our children.

Our friend David, whom we only call when
we don't really have enough time to talk, says:
Are you two married yet? He is quirky-alone
in a Minneapolis tenement. He's given up
his love affair with book writing. Quell it,
he says. We get ten years, he says. Ten years
or two cars. Either win or grow up. Give up
this body of work, he says. It cannot love.

We get sick with some Romantic affliction.
For weeks we moon around the old house:
sleeping-in, doing errands with Dad, stuck
in some regressive adolescent funk.
We break into our father's bourbon.
We say: We must burn this empty gesture
at its open mouth. We say: Well said!

We mean: This is no way to make meaning.
Our father shows up in his bathrobe,
so we pass him the bottle. Look, he says:
If Love is the sicker of two sick,
sick puppies, what choice do we have?
We must bring it home and fix it.

CARETAKER

I'm in charge of this mustard brown vase and so far I'm not doing a very good job. It's not precious or pretty, but I like it and I'm supposed to protect it. I keep conjuring up quotidian errands and minor distractions, like not only do I have to pee, I have to shelve all these issues of *US Weekly*, and whenever I get sidetracked by text messages that say things like, "Satan is looking through your window right now, so *dance*, fool," a small monkey swings down from the chandelier and chips my vase with a ball-peen hammer. *Le sigh*. Once again, I go collect all the porcelain chips and stash them under my tongue. I'm always doing this: failing at a task then trying to protect the part I ruined, like something might hatch of my mistake. Which is why I just wander off to the bar with the jigsaw puzzle of a vase in my mouth. When I get there the stools are occupied by every adjunct professor I've ever met. Gray-faced, they turn in unison to ask, "Karyna, why did you flake again?" I can't open my mouth, so I just shrug and the bartender hands me the husk of my first-generation iMac, heavy with a decade of dust. There's a family of fruit flies dying in my wine. I'm supposed to recover my explication of Keats' "Ode on a Grecian Urn," and if I can just keep my shit together for one last deep scan, I think, I can defrag the contract I broke with my readers long before any of us were born.

SENSUAL VOCABULARY

"The phonaesthetics of *cellar door* . . ." begins the poetry professor we're all crushing on hard, who hovers lustily over these linguistic deep-tracks like none of us has seen *Donnie Darko*—as if he, bare-handed, built the traditional English farmhouse and its slanted semantic trapdoors. "Spare in clusters," he croons. "So full of liquids." It's tempting to eroticize the automaton, to resuscitate the word-machine, bleeding capital into the Speakeasy of Language: "Look down my rain barrel, slide down my cellar door, and we'll be jolly friends forever more, more, one two three four, shut the door." If Romantics persist, so must cellars, and snaking lines of poets at their doors, velvet ropes, burlap sacks for the sensual vocabulary sold there, big barrels of words—both Latinate and Anglo Saxon—scoops stuck in them. *What would you like?* Three blackberries, a *whirr*, a wax cylinder, one oleander, a cacophonous horde spangled in swallows, ripe figs wallowing in limpid pools, a mélange of moss, a soupçon of snark. Take the word *austere*, for instance. It does not mean what it should: cool blonde baroness from Vienna. The best words always lie and are more expensive than the rest: vermillion, dearth, crepuscular, droll, flush, nonplussed, scurrilous, chartreuse, yardarm, hoi polloi. Here's our sack of fragrant manure. Here we are in line at the cellar door. Consider the following words carefully: *speak, easy*. Watch us spit the password in a palm, see us smear it across the lintel and load up our word-sacks to squander again, like Death can't read what we write about her, can't even find our damn house on a map, so blinded by our song and austerity.

ARS POETICA IN A BOAT (WITH YOU)

Lost Tom, the oldest orphan, watching you
from the reeds on the banks of the river—
sneering through his wild slap of strawberry
blond, like, *you've come back then, have you?*
Wave cordially, but understand:
he will never wave back. If you say his name
he'll spit it out & set the gators on you,
he'll puff up with bile & blacken the blossoms.
The past. He wonders what you want with it now:
to splice it, sell it, set fire to the archives?
Let the original cut rot in its canister?
He cleans his nails with a bowie knife.
A pretty still, but you know things
are not so bucolic. Come night, he will lead
the black mass of orphans on paper horses
of your own poor construction. They will
follow along the banks so you can't berth
your little craft. Their torchlight will swell
& multiply & eat all your oxygen & it will
suck at the paper leaves & paper steeds until
they are black in the blackness & you smell
his knife melting like the prop it is & there is,
truly, nothing to write about but the fire
(you must admit) I started in the first place.

SELF-PORTRAIT AS EROTIC THRILLER

Natasha in her underwear on an old floral chair.
Feet on the armrest. Look at her.
Little sensual snail. Smoke in the sunlight.
Now she is a passenger in his red Wagoneer.
Feet on the dashboard. The same sunlight.
They race to a lakeside house replete
with Adirondacks and loons where someone is bound
to die. In a Coeur d'Alene diner
their waitress is pretty with big breasts and black eyes.
She deserves better than this.
When she goes out by the dumpster to smoke
they kidnap her. *Look at me*, says Natasha. *Look.*

Cut to sunlight on the empty dock.
Grilled meat smell licking the side of the lake.
Three figures in a Chester Yawl.
Natasha feeds the waitress wedges of apple
off the side of a knife. The waitress wears an
old green bikini. Natasha is nude. One of them
wears a necklace. A speedboat slices through
the no wake zone. A spray of water in the sunlight.
The droplets cling to their sunglasses. No one
wipes them away. *Look*, says Natasha.
We all have an imperfect past.
For instance, says the Man, *I like to yank*
necklaces from women's throats. I am unconcerned
whether I break the clasps or the women.
    . . . Does this make me a monster?

They swim out to the untethered raft.
The Man is showing off. He dives down under
the cool shadow, hides between rusted barrels.
He looks through the gray planks
into the women's green and cherry crotches.

Sunlight. He puts algae in his hair. He gurgles.
Look, giggles the waitress, *the Monster*.
A thing goes ping, ping, ping.
His mouth. Her ear. Someone makes a wineglass sing.
A spray of pearls in the sunlight. No comment.
Natasha puts her thumb between her lips.
She can't stop this. No, she *won't*.
The camera is underwater, sinking fast.
No sounds now. Wavery sunlight above.
Two silhouettes, watching it happen.

Cut to October.
A body washes up in a greening slip.
It's waxen with cold and axes down
everyone's Indian summer. A saxophone
solo purls around the bruised breasts
igniting a sickening bloom of desire
we recognize in the new sheriff's eyes.

SEVENTIES COUCH

Well then, here we are:
packing our separate books into separate boxes.
You don't want to make this easy:
the toy ships and animal figurines—
taken down, one by one,
silenced in noisy swathes of tissue.
I deface the hot windows with whorls of soap.

Small boxes taped, you take a break,
take out your guitar, mask my tattered heart
in minor chords. We move the couch
to the curb with a sign: *Free to good home!*

Later, all the cushions are gone
but the brown husk is still there:
stupid, obdurate, utterly useless.
And I am so *pissed*—at the homeless man,
or whoever has spirited away our cushions,
and moreover, at the heavy-handed metaphor:
you and me out on the curb
with this cumbersome orphan of the seventies—
this thing no one can plausibly adopt.

It's so hot it just has to rain. It *has* to.
We're listening to Jim Croce's "Operator"
on ~~our~~ rediscovered stereo.
I'm watching you, irritable in your blue T-shirt,
a roll of masking tape around your wrist.

You loathe Jim Croce, but you're trying not to.
He reminds you of doing errands with your dad,
and you just want to spackle all
these stupid holes in relative peace.

"Hey," I say. "If you had to listen to *one* song
for the *rest* of your life . . ."
You're already groaning. I keep going.
"Would it be Stevie Wonder's 'I Just Called to Say I Love You,'
Lionel Richie's 'Hello,' or Jim Croce's 'Operator'?"
I know you won't answer. You hate this game.

Instead, you want to know how Jim Croce died.
Neither of us can remember,
but you're pretty sure he died of the seventies.
"Jim, I'm sorry," you say,
"but we're going to the eighties soon and, well . . .
you can't come. Just sit on this brown couch
and someone will come get you."

I laugh till I sob and still you won't stop this.
You go out to smoke. I can see you perched
on the stern of the couch like it's about to set sail—
all those blossoms spackling your forearm, you *fool*.

PARLOR

LAST GIRL ON THE FLOOR

If she dances alone in her kitchen at night, maybe she's afraid
      there are men with guns
            out there in the dark
                  looking into her bright fishbowl.

If so, she should
            give them a show, but she shouldn't
                give them a still target.

                          If she is a disappointment
        "as a girl"

it's because she doesn't know when to leave
      the party. And if people suddenly
          "forget" to invite her,

                      she should try not to steal
their little blue
            decorative
                seashell soaps.

And if she's good at manipulation?
      She should try body isolations instead.
          Give 'em a neck roll, make her hips go

                Bang, Bang.

          Tut & tilt, dip & pin
& then
in the middle of everybody's favorite song, just
                    freeze.

          If she can hold this pose &
          if she can *keep* holding it—
          maybe she can become

the spindle

the single pin around which
the whole party platter spins.

If she can hold this pose &
if she can *keep* holding it—
maybe she can become

the hole

in the record itself & when
her hosts begin to yawn &
even the gay boys are gone

the beat drops, but it's just her

bad self doubled in the bay window,

a shatter of glass as she shoots herself

with a finger.

COSTUMES REQUIRED

A chocolate-bartering devil skims
into the Halloween party uninvited
& undeterred. I think: *that man*
will pluck something from me.

Granite counters, laminate floors,
ten guys named Steve who only
talk to each other. Me doing
my best Sally Bowles act again.

Wearing little more than a wig,
a tuxedo vest & a good sweat,
I catch my silvered reflection
in the open fridge & wince.

Michigan winter comes, too,
blowing its preseason shave ice
all over the windows, dropping
off its slush pile in the dark hall.

I go downstairs for a cigarette
with some moll brandishing
a cardboard machine gun
encrusted in black glitter.

It immediately flies away—
flick-flacks down the street sanded
over in cold, diamante white.
We can't tell where the smoke ends

& our breath begins. But here he is:
the chocolate-bartering devil,
who slides down the banister
& out into the night to pitch me.

What worries me is not that
I sell my soul to Beelzebub
at a Halloween party, but how
hard I barter for it: scripting

the terms with a red Sharpie
he's got hanging from his horn—
scanning for loopholes, soldering
them shut with faux legalese.

After I sign, he snatches his ledger.
Thank you for doing business, he says,
crossing my palm with no less than
I expect: a gold-foiled Godiva rose.

He slides on his soles down the
new-snowed street. The moll & I,
nipples hard as bullets & mouths
full of chocolate, reascend the loft.

At midnight I win "Sluttiest Costume."
I try to explain Weimar Berlin, but during
my victory dance, ten guys named Steve
keep strangling me with my own boa.

YOU ARE MY NEW GOD

I know this because I so wanna dance in your chorus.
Wanna whisper dirt so sweet in your ear
the center of 1989 will rot and fall out, and through
that hole, an eleven-year-old me will see her True Name
on the nape of your neck and know how to breakdance.
Look, I think I've been learning this sidestroke
all my life to slam-dunk my apple in your basket
and really rock out in this Slow Lagoon with you.
And I wanna be so Girl for you that I get all, "Yeah!"
with my bubblegum baby-making machine,
like I wanna mermaid up inside your Cultural Memory
to fight off Tom Hanks and Hasbro. Boy, you're
a roast beef sandwich dipped in Drakkar Noir
and I wanna fly up inside your Men's Grooming Kit
and *die* there so I know how it feels to be your *thing*:
cedar-scented and clipped with safety scissors.
And then I wanna get so lost in your Man Cave,
I need you to invent a New Legend for the map
made of footprints that will teach me to foxtrot
where I bend over the Hot Oven in my butter-
colored frock and make muffins that make
muffins that make banana nut muffins
and rename me in a pile of your Sweet Laundry
that is so dirty but won't do itself, *Dumpling*.

SWING DANCERS NAMED MICHAEL

You don't understand: it made my polka dots quiver & flash so fiercely, I stole a pair of T-strap shoes & disappeared in the Swing Underground. It was seething with dancers named Michael. They hoofed & hollered & when they danced together they made baby dancers named Michael who jangled out of them & joined in the gummy moans & scratches of hot jazz—how could I help but bring gifts for the Michaels? Fat scarves, fingerless gloves, red globe grapes, keys to garden apartments. And if my gift was *very* generous, the Michaels stood me in the center of the floor & swung around the axis of me. My petticoats swelled in their proximity & the power of man-on-man dancing put finger waves in my hair, moved my beauty mark from cheek to cheek. I grew dizzy. They were simply *divine*. But did you know the name Michael is an impossible question? It means, "Who is like God?" And how do you answer when there are so many Michaels? The Archangel, *yes*—but also the Drunkard, the Swimmer, the Pop Star, the Stammerer, the Boxer & the Documentarian. My Michaels were none of these things, but dear *God*— the miracles they made with negative space. Like the time I stood in the dance floor's hotspot & a voice in the dark cried, *"Get her, Michael!"* One of them shimmied down the floor for me & *golly gee*, some holy ragdoll (I thought I'd sold) shook out of me shining in two-tone shoes & began to Begin the Beguine.

SELF-PORTRAIT AS AGING STARLET

Swaddled in gold lamé ruffles, an ingénue in a bassinette.
Her birth certificate already reads, "Costumes by *Irene*."
Poor baby doll! Whose star will she hitch her little, red
wagon to? Someone leaves the nursery window open.
Calendar pages flip up & fly off. One minute she's nursing
Shirley Temples; next thing you know, it's splitsville with
Mickey Rooney. The cards are stacked. She practices her
fast talk, her girl sleuth, her smear. A starter bungalow
opens on its hinges. She dates a hit parade of fellows for
the next fifteen years. The chainmail on her seltzer bottle
grows rusty before she learns what it means to love.
She shoplifts leotards, draws the batwing brow, smokes.
Jacqueline Susann, pink & well-thumbed on her vanity.
She awakes with a start: she forgot to have a baby. She has
a Bellini instead. Time passes: a chorus line of champagne
bubbles. The glam rockers move in. All too soon,
Challenger rains its heavy metal all over her garden.
She bathes in TV light, eats a whole turtle cheesecake.
The funk dies, a skunk dies in her kidney-shaped
swimming pool. An '80s Rich Kid's House falls open on its
gingerbread hinges. She awakes with a start: she forgot
to buy a fax machine. She buys an Ogilvie Home Perm
instead. About the time she's decided to reinvent herself,
she knocks over a mannequin, shatters its swan neck.
She can't afford to replace it. It's too late to sweet-talk her
way out of this spray tan. I saw her just last week,
facedown on my driveway. When I suggested she change
her name, she let out a shriek to beat the Big Band Sound.

The man in the first row says, *Gimme a girl who smokes red cigarettes while asking us occupational questions.* So I ash into his hat brim & say, What do you do, sir? Do you like being profiled by the entertainment police? The man hands me his bowler & says, *Gimme Liza in a backless vest perched on top of a chair.* So I draw him a picture of a glam mantis gone to seed & bookmark *The Unbearable Lightness of Being.* Here, I say, will *this* satisfy your lust for Prague? A woman in back says, *Sorry, we meant Magritte.* So I spackle my face with sky-colored greasepaint. The third row says, *But we're suckers for the phrase "candy apple red."* Fuck it, I say. They glitter with sweat & applause. *Now,* says the emcee, *I will strap you into a torpedo bra & staple you with flaming sheets of Prufrock.* Okay, I say, after the auto-da-fé will paper ephemera be collected in my memory? My audience goes, *Oh, no, no, no, oh, no, but you will wake up & wonder, "Where is that steamer trunk I kept my best vocabulary in?" & we will pretend not to know.* I say, Audience, O Audience! Why do you seek to destroy me? The man in the first row says, *This has become very tiresome. Give us the girl who smokes red cigarettes again.* Okay, I say, pass me the ashtray. *That "ashtray,"* he harrumphs, *happens to be my wife.* The emcee says, *Give us a French doll with removable britches!* So I put on Jelly Roll's "Black Bottom Stomp" & crisscross my lavender stockings. Look at me, I say. My doll parts move! A silence. The woman in back says, *It's just that you make us all very uncomfortable.*

WET BAR

WAITING FOR GREG O.

In the weeks before Greg and his band come down for SXSW
    we have a love affair with him in our heads.
Adam wants to get his hair cut by this guy he found on Yelp
    because he thinks he's too old for his hairstyle. Like, maybe
he's the Fat Dad at the skating rink who doesn't know he's creepy?
We google Men's Hairstyles. The High-and-Tight? The Fauxhawk?
The Pompadour? The Modified Skrillex? It's not even funny.
What could anyone possibly ask for with a straight face?
In the car on the way to brunch, Adam loses it.
    "Here's the thing," he says. "If you're not short-chinned,
    thick-haired, high-cheekboned, and/or Asian, you're *screwed*."
And maybe that's true, but Greg is coming regardless, and the restaurant
    is a farmyard of freshly shorn bros in neon sunglasses.
Bros are bros, Greg's in a band, but what are *we*? Thirtysomething
    semi-alcoholics who don't know how to make new friends.
We buy a bathroom scale and start losing weight
    without explicitly stating why:
visions of Greg dogsledding down from the wooly North!
Three weeks later, we get the call:
Greg's staying in a hotel outside town and won't be coming tonight,
    but *surely* tomorrow night.
We stare at each other: embarrassed, angry. Back at the bar:
Adam, hot & verbose, his Yelp hairdo perched
    like an impotent bowler upon his outrage,
    going, "And the *other* thing that pisses me off is . . ."
Me nodding sourly into my beer, saying
    "Starfucker, starfucker, starfucker."
We grow silent. We have wasted our Wednesday.
"Maybe we should just move to Montreal," Adam says.
We drink to that but won't look each other in the eye.
We cannot move. Our phones are dark in our pockets.

WHAT HAPPENS IN 1918 WON'T STAY IN 1918

Her students say "nothing new" because they read it somewhere.
She tells them to recycle. Jealousy is a kind of arthritis.
She feels it in her hands when they make things.
Here is a white girl who calls her headband creations "Oriental."
Here is a white boy who growls around campus on his restored Indian.
Here is a couple in the commons sharing a Red Baron pizza.
Here is a class shadow play: the *Carpathia* sinking into paper waves.
Finger puppets, cute and gruesome: the Romanov family, shot.
Claude Debussy, dead. Wilfred Owen, *doomed*.
Guillaume Apollinaire leading a charge of zombie Spanish flu victims.

She dreams her students reintroduce sex to the public sphere.
They hang it from giant chandeliers. But she is hysterical—
a wandering womb in a grass-stained hobble skirt.
Her syntax is a croquet mallet she swings unpredictably.
They strap her to the bed. They don't understand
what she needs. Still, they stand vigil.
Their cinematic eyes never stray far. "Precociousness . . ."
she mumbles, "is the name of this mutiny."
She shows them *Battleship Potemkin*. They break into her
liquor cabinet. Round after round of White Russians.

                     They get drunk and rename her Alexandra.

THIS IS A SCREWDRIVER, SHE SAYS

pouring something called Smirnoff
into my Sunny-D and telling me
terrible things I can never unknow.
We get tired of Uno.
It's too hot, she says, and undresses,
room damp with the open-mouthed
memory of her ton of sleeping brothers—
a smell I can put my finger in:
sweet socks and peppered ham.
They share this mattress.
But they aren't home.
She stretches out in bluebell panties.
The window AC drips in my drink.
Thunder mutters in the distance.
She opens her legs. *You lost*, she says,
so this is your punishment.
Ew, I say, but I want to, and do.
Then it's time for her punishment.
Up above, the heavy cloud of her
teddy hammock threatens to burst.
We hear a door slam. We scuttle
to the closet. In the dark we're even
closer. My face in her crotch
and an old pair of Converse.
I don't think we can ever stop this.
But it's raining and her brothers
come back in from the court.
The closet opens and they catch us at it
like unearthed worms.
One of them throws a ball at us.
She curses at them in Spanish.
You raped our sister, says the tall one.
He looks like he believes it.
I try to find my shorts as they spit

and kick me. I'm so dizzy.
She was my friend. We were eleven.

LOTTERY OF BAD APOLOGIES

Maybe I threw a lamp at your head,
but you're the one who broke it.
You could have ducked, but you didn't.
I'm sorry you have terrible timing.
I'm sorry you can't take a joke.
I warned you I was working
but you kept yap-yap-yapping.
I was a black rubber mallet mid-swing
& you were a menagerie of glass figurines:
pouting princesses & nickering ponies
& they were in my way. I'm sorry if
you *felt* that way, but my anger was
the lesser crime. It's a question of taste.
You slapped me first. You hid my keys
so I would hate you. I hit you
because I loved you. You're lucky
I don't leave you.
I pinned you to the counter.
I made you my cheesecake. Can you
blame me for destroying a cheesecake?
Can you blame my knife for nicking
the vein of your strawberry swirl?
My blood sugar was low & I'm sorry
but *frankly*? You were being a bitch.
You were baiting me. I'd barely slept.
You don't know how to pick your battles.
I blame the gin. It's genetic.
I was never meant to be monogamous.
You're borderline. I'm sorry I'm
a "bad friend." Besides, I told you
I just wanted to sleep. *I just want to
sleep*, I said. You know I don't like to
repeat myself. I saw your mouth moving,
not speaking. I had to set fire to the footage

so no one else would see it & know
that I made you this way: square
& silver, a clothes rack in a nightclub.
I bought you fake wings & made you
wear them. I tore them off so you would
know you were not a butterfly, but you
were the one who did the Disco of Becoming.
I was unbecoming. I was a tiled floor.
But you were a liar, a busted blender.
So what if I liked your blood flicked across me?
Can you blame me for bringing some color
to my high-traffic areas? You tried to be "helpful"
but I covered my ears: *La-la-la-la-la-la-la!*
I can't *hear* you, I said. This is my house, I said.
You just *live* here. You're high maintenance.
I hope you're happy with yourself.
This is what happens, I said. You're histrionic.
If it's any consolation, I hate myself.
I work all the time because *one* of us has to.
What do you think my stress says about *you*?
Stop hovering, I said. Your breath stinks.
You know I can't stand it when you ask,
"Can I ask you a question?"
I'm not Wikipedia. Why are those words
so important to you? We were both mad.
Things were said, but if you just
have to hear it, I'm *sorry*, okay?
I was pissed & pissing in the wind.
You were wind chimes. I was a birch cane.
You made too much noise
so I broke you. I'm sorry
that I couldn't bear you.

IT IS EASIER

this way—a rushing, a fluttered grunt,
streaking through the house as if you were
always ten minutes behind yourself—
than to answer her. To answer her asks
a full stop. An honest assessment.
The dark rot of a jailbroken walnut
under your shoe. To stop and try
to piece it together. It is the worst work.
It is easier to be sorry than to fix it.
There she is: knees up on the green silk couch,
as if only one detail, among many.
Her eyes are open parentheses.
You are causing a great deal of pain.
It is easier to continue, add on
than to stop, exclude. There:
the nut, the girl on the green silk couch.
Crack it or cut it out. Make a goodbye
pie, a reparation pie. Stop, do it slow.
This is the worst work. It is also the only.

LOVE IN THE AGE OF BAR PARAPHERNALIA

When he turns down a sip of her green Chartreuse
he might as well close the book on her.
This stuff she's been huffing from her snifter
sours, turns to love-thinner. Her mentor:

Look, I can't be your lover. This is far too easy
to parse. She stuffs it down
into her Dior—*je comprends, je comprends.*

Trapped in this fern bar, swiveling
between a player piano and a Wit who won't
love her back, she fingers an amber
ashtray, then drops it, like it might free the fossilized
beetles of her best words. Nothing comes out.
No glissandi of glass, just two dull halves.

There in the mirror, a dumbshow. She hangs
from his tenterhooks like a macramé owl.
She drags the lacy hem of her embarrassment
around the melting ice sculpture, up and down
his classical syntax—it's almost romantic
to examine the situation at some remove:
his heart on her finger, a dried-out contact.
She shines it on his shirt, puts it back in.

Why did you do that? he says.
I'll do anything, she says, fanning her
shame away with the cocktail list.

and suddenly the place is flooded with search lights and Mellencamp. Men with boring haircuts pick up plastic deer, shake the spare keys out, put them down. They've got you bike-chained to the picnic table because you're the prime suspect. Because somebody told *somebody* that you're the type of person who leaves their suitcase unattended at the airport. All the detectives are drunk; it's Oktoberfest. Between interrogations, they pound on the table, demanding meats and puddings. "What is your occupation?" asks a man with a sweaty red mustache. "Adjunct Professor," you tell him. "What subject do you teach?" asks a man who looks eight-months pregnant. "Freshman Composition," you answer. Their lips quiver like bowstrings and you can tell that the facts have not fallen in your favor. It's as if they've had a collective epiphany: all their lives you've been tricking them into too-tight pants. "I don't have a *motive*," you tell them as they check the box on the form that says that you do.

Then Ethan says I'm working the hell-on-wheels librarian look today.
More *specifically*, he says, a New York City Public *Library* librarian
who's nursing a Vicodin/vodka hangover and has no time for *anyone*.
Immanuel Kant? Find it yourself, bitch. There's a system for a *reason*.

Michelle says, but that *belt*? Not so much. You've *got* to lose the belt.
Then Jon says, what is that like your fourth cigarette in the last *hour*?
I start to say no but then remember how Kevin's always saying that
I extrapolate from my own experience, and I'm like, *jee-zus*, Kevin!

Whose experience *should* I extrapolate from? Or is extrapolation itself
the problem? I'm sitting at the bar trying not to smoke or extrapolate
but then the conversation returns to my outsized belt and Ethan says,
you've become a living extension of your poetry; you do its *bidding*.

Michelle says, listen, don't be offended, we're not criticizing your *style*.
Laura snorts and asks, who would *dare*? There's a *reason* we call you
Karyna "Shut-the-Fuck-Up" McGlynn. Michelle applies a fresh slash
of lipstick. *Whatever*, she says. We're *line*-editing your outfit, that's all.

THE NEW SINCERITY

Adam says he *can't* because he's trapped in a sleepy mimosa dungeon. We're full of champagne & starch & can't rise up out of ourselves. It takes us ten minutes to remember the word "glib." Thinking is like climbing into a short-sheeted bed: familiar enough, but *I don't know— just fucking Wiki it when we get home?* A character on one of our Hulu shows tells another character, "I think you've been watching too many '80s sitcoms on Hulu." I'm supposed to believe we live in a world where fifteen-year-olds know the theme song to *The Jeffersons?* I guess *Gossip Girl* grants us brief economic reprieve, but Adam says he misses the halcyon days of crab rangoon & non-ironic corduroy. When we go out drinking on Easter, there's a bevy of UT law students. One guy is wearing pastel pink chinos & loafers with no socks. After three pecan porters I can't help myself: I go tell the guy, *This is a little weird but I have this blog where I blog about one Totally Awesome Thing every day, so I was wondering if I could take a picture of you for my blog? Because I think your pink pants are Totally Awesome.* The whole party breaks into cheers & back slaps. One bro tries to start "For He's a Jolly Good Fellow," but fails. Pink Pants asks, *Can I run to my Land Rover real quick?* He returns sporting a plaid cardigan & his preppiest pout: To Be Young & Rich is Pure *Misery*, by Ralph Lauren. I tell myself this is something I do in the name of New Sincerity. At 4 a.m. I wake to the sound of Adam retching in the bathroom. I curl up outside the door & tell him about my dream where C+C Music Factory was an *actual* factory, where "Gonna Make You Sweat" (Everybody Dance Now)" was our one earnest anthem. It played on repeat all night long. We knew every word. We worked there.

BATH

RENTED CONFESSIONAL

You try to write the truth but it makes you miserable,
like throwing a book into a bubble bath.
"I confess!" you yell, and bid your words
make wine-dark angels on the snowy carpet of discourse.
The undertaking smells like humdrum brimstone,
but you cannot determine the source of the smell.
There is no country song at the heart
of your tiny mansion, just a scribbling sound
from the basement, like a child punishing himself
for a crime he knows he didn't really commit.
You try to find the source of the scribbling,
but wherever you go someone is there
to switch on the floodlights or flip up the floorboards.
It's a ruinous sort of hide-and-seek in which
the hider goes to live in another house,
or disappears altogether. You try tracking
the cabernet footprints, but they make circles and come
to baffling inconclusions: the landing of the stairs,
the side of a loveseat, a Jacuzzi full
of lukewarm lavender water, and bits of mortar.

BOMB THREAT

Adam, I am big & pregnant in the tub,
& you are back in Massachusetts—
going up in the flames of New Love
all over Yankee Candle. Between my legs
bobs the bomb. It will flense the world
of our atheistic blubber. I shape the thing—
patting the whitish clay of me, smoothing
the head with a palmful of bathwater
& I know what you would tell me:
Get out of there! But this is the epicenter.
Me & my nesting doll: we are safe—see how, *boom*,
the destruction radiates out, leaves me alone.
What did you say about history's senators
knifing the ones they embrace? There is an ordinance
I don't remember. Something's changed. I'm flattened.
The drained tub ticks with mollusks & lobsters.
They make a racket against the clean porcelain
while you are out huffing all of New England
& not here to tell me otherwise, Yank.
What should I do about it: the stopped clock
in the corner & its giant grandfather clause.

OUVRIR

I wasn't really what he wanted
because I was always closed—
Even when I was sure I'd turned the sign on.
Even when I thought I was conducting business.
I guess it was a shady kind of business:
a jewelry store with metal shutters.
I told him I wasn't a night bus full of people
you could just look right up into.
He told me my eyes sucked up
all the oxygen in the room
but didn't use that breath to express anything,
that I'd never been truly naked,
or seen a naked person in my life.
He said, What do you *feel*?
And I said, Nothing.
But he tried to wedge his foot
in the closing door of my mouth,
so I said I felt like an albino fish
in a sphere of water, no bowl—
which seemed to me like Certain Death.
I hated the way he smiled at me then,
like he loved my psychosis.
He said maybe I was more like
a wreath-shaped Jell-O mold
with fruit inside. I said he wanted
to put his hands in me and ruin me
for a fucking maraschino. He said
my metaphor-making was reckless
and rooted in fear. The last place we went
he tried to open the door for me.
I can do it myself, I said.
But I couldn't. The café was closed.
Turned away, something inside my
see-thru *yes* shook its little head.

MILK BATH

There's something under the snow I want.
No use digging. I only want this one bone:
his bed, abstract under its seam of black ice.

I'm hungry. He tells me to wait.

Ok. I float home through the snow.
Shapes climb from wasting drifts. A big dog
opens one eye behind an invisible fence.

If I crossed over, we could hasten the end of this.

I'm watching Polish porn: the star, Ewa Sonnet,
submerged in a bathtub full of milk. Her breasts
buoy up, overwhelming and gold before lapsing
into the consummate opacity of her bath.
I watch this scene five times:
the gentle slosh, the bland pop.

I'm hungry. Do I want to have her? Be her?
I suspect something subterranean, violent.

All winter I wait for him to want me.
Look, he says, an animal makes a hole in the snow
and waits. So I wait. Violets pulse
like shrapnel through the crust, drifts break
down overnight. The salt remains.

Rewind: Ewa Sonnet in her clawfoot tub.
Her breasts like two surfacing submarines
in an arctic sea, steaming up, up.
Milk sluicing off the hulls, beading her
nipples. Bigger, bigger.
Spring's killer striptease.

April now: from winter's grip comes the defunct
husk of a bashed-in boombox, animal bones,
VHS tape crushed with a boot heel.

He stands in his sunlit room. I drop my dress.
He says, Memory, if we're lucky, is the one thing
we'll never recover from.

FIRST-AID KIT

He sits me on the toilet in the dark beach house,
      extracts a fang of beer glass from my foot.
It's so warm the smell & hiss of peroxide is promising me
love, *love*—   I won't sit still.

It's always the same:
I twirl over the surface of the world as if
      it's an even plane of polished pine.
    No loose boards.   No rusty nails.

Then he is tending me, laying out his tools,
taking hold of my paw in this dumbshow: *okay, stop.*

When we drove up the Pacific Coast Highway,
      the splendor kept buckling impossibly on itself.
Between the ocean & the poppies on the cliff side,
I remember thinking: now, *now* is the best moment of my life.
Then we would round the bend—no, *now*, it's *now*.
    Nature kept trumping herself endlessly.
        Can I say I thought I would *die* of pleasure?

Barefoot & drunk on the beach, we play a game.
Even though I'm losing, I say, *Connect four*—
      He just smiles, bemused by the black out,
              my little rebellions of red.
    Racing him to the bar, it bites me.

The world isn't an even playing field, he says.
    I know this.   It's a night breeze
sliding in on the blade of his knife in my foot.

BLUE-EYED BOYFRIENDS

Every blue-eyed boyfriend lining up
to look at me all at once: a firing squad
of looking, my head in one of those
big paper cones to keep a bitch
from biting her wounds, hackles up
against the levee, hemmed by the bayou.
All my blue-eyed boyfriends swaying
silent as spikerush, staring me down.
Some without socks, grown stockier,
self-effacing, shit-faced. Doesn't matter.
They just want to see me *see* them.
Their eyes—some wet, shallow, shiny
as pie pans left in the rain, some pure
pupil, so bottomless-inkwell I can't see
the blue until it smudges my thumb.
Some for a second, like looking through
the sunroof between tall buildings.
Others so light they look blighted
by lime, bleached of gravity. What now?
I throw nickels at them in remuneration.
They *ping* off the pylons or *platt*
tail-up onto the sludge of the bayou.
All my ammunition gone, I finally get it.
I take out my make-up mirror:
the eye of the storm, bloodshot,
rimmed in blue and contraflow.
The forecast funnels in: I know, I *know*.

~~EYEBROWS~~

Ethan calls to say his date remembers me
from drama school. "Oh!" she says.
"Karyna! The one with no eyebrows!"
He reports this in good humor, but the specter
of my hairless face rises like Munch's scream.
It's true: I once had no eyebrows.
I shaved them off, drew them back on,
wore wigs, went to drama school,
& worshiped Marlene Dietrich.
"Her name is Opal," Ethan says.
I know exactly who he means—
she used to stand in front of me
in Movement for Actors. She had
an orchard tattooed across her back.
"From *Into the Woods*," she said.
You could get lost in it. There was even a wolf.
I tell Ethan about the time she got me drunk
& took me to get a Sappho tattoo on my wrist:
I sobered up in the chair & chickened out.
I told Opal, "*Real* actresses aren't inked."
(I'm surprised this isn't what she remembers.)
I wanted to be made & scraped clean & remade
every night. "I told her I was a *palimpsest*, Ethan."
He, of all people, should understand—
the men who fell prey to my bizarre charms
slept in the bouncy castles of their own
amorphous sexualities. I want to remind him
how I once stuck a pin in the balloon
of my long-term relationship in order to be
drunk & excellent & eyebrowless with him
in the bad light of a Sheraton bathroom—
watching him fuck me in the mirror,
watching him already regret it,
watching my eyebrows sweat off—

but Ethan's laughing now: "Seriously? *A palimpsest?*
Opal's right. You were *totally* pretentious."
I hang up the phone but it's too late:
I'm beside myself, back in drama school,
doing *A Doll's House* for a dozen natural girls
who keep giving each other that arch look,
like I still don't know the right way to act.

BASEMENT

RICH GIRL CAMP REVENGE FANTASY

We all know where you're from & where you're going
in your dingy wind shorts & knockoff Keds:
the rival tribe's hillside, fired up in the night.

Stop stealing our hair ties.
Just shake the spirit stick like you give a shit.

After taps, not even a flashlight,
ass-deep in the creek, you give the Houston girls
a body scrub & check *down there* for leeches.

We're just making *s'mores*.
But you call it a Witch Picnic & put a pox on our ponies.

You're the one who's allergic to yarn.
You're the one who gets bloody noses & can't clean the cabin.
You're the kickball spaz, the K-Mart kid
who wants too badly to climb in our war canoe.

It's after reveille & we can't find our shower shoes.
You're ruining this for everybody!

Snake in the drain, you say. *Dead girl's ghost in the cypress*.
You've started a séance & can't come to chapel.

You say you want to
get our occult loins going like diving boards
& string us up
in the fume noose of our own puff-paints.

Now the counselors can't find you.
We know you're smoking with grounds crew
at the edge of the range where the dark belongs
to *the three-legged maniacal gnasher!*

Where care package trash & dirty words
spill out on the grass with splintered arrows.

You're not even *good* at nature!
With your sneer & your bowl cut.

The PA pages & pages you. You pretend not to hear.
You're up in the branches clutching a pitcher
of barbeque sauce. Below, our parents snake
through the oaks in a line of seersucker
& clean, white Suburbans.

FORTUNE IS A WOMAN IN FURS AT THE FOOD BANK

There are countless ways to dig up and diss the girl
I used to be, but the best and most heartbreaking
is the one where I drive my French Vanilla Lexus
to the food bank on First Hill and park it right in front.
Because I can. I'm late for drama class. Dark glasses,
bottle-blonde Veronica Lake do, sometimes even
a cheetah-print coat. I give my name and zip code,
go get in line behind women with gaggles of kids.
They take everything they are offered. I do not.
I have shaved my eyebrows off and drawn them back on.
A food bank is not really like a bank. It's a horseshoe
of makeshift tables, each with a different genre of food.
My favorite genre is the one at the top of the horseshoe:
baked goods—rosemary focaccia, everything bagels,
only-slightly-squashed sourdough. And the men
who volunteer there, who seem poorer than me,
take great delight in giving me whole cakes.
"Hey, baby, I've been saving this turtle cheesecake
all day, just for you." How sometimes I'll take it
and sometimes I won't, just to spite them.
Just to show them a thing or two about luxury.

ELEGIAC STANZAS (WITH RHINESTONES)

Let me tell you how Princess Di died for me.
Here's the news surging across the Atlantic,
gathering force as it sweeps over the Bible belt,
comes hurtling down I-35 on the back of a semi,
slipping through the tinted double doors
on a stolen snatch of sunlight, coming to rest
at the Crystal Palace Gentleman's Club.

I have just offered a well-dressed man a lap dance.
He rebuffs me with a polite, but firm
"No thank you. I'm waiting for Big Tits."
Like he's waiting for the bus.
This is my sixth Diet Coke with extra cherries
and I'm sitting at a little lacquer table
with an engineer who shyly strokes
the black feathers of my open negligee.

But the news: zipping over the carpet's
neon geometry, strobing from stiletto
to stiletto in a crude game of telephone,
until, finally, one of the older girls, Misty,
in a turmoil of mascara, rushes my table,
crushes herself into me and chokes it out:
"Princess Di . . . she's been . . . *shot!*"

Look, I can never make it sound right,
or convince anyone this isn't about me,
because however I tell it, there I am
in a San Antonio strip club dressing room,
singularly unaffected amidst the glitter
and wails, while girls I'd never spoken to
held me to their bare breasts
and just sobbed. All the men were left
weirdly alone with their wallets,

and the manager, against his wishes,
had to shut down the Palace and send
his inconsolable princesses home.

OF ALL THE DEAD PEOPLE I KNOW

I can't imagine any of them hanging out.
They are in arcadia with their laptops
but there are no outlets, and they are
playing a game in which they
can never move to the next level.

Except for the grandmothers, who are
rifling through bins of discount clothing,
looking for a deal on something they lost.

It must be so lonely. Selling shoes
for eternity, never learning any new jokes.

We need a new imagination when it comes
to death. If only for our own sake. I'm tired
of imagining the dead sitting on swings
with no one in the world to push them.

MORTIFICATION MONTAGE

She writes her mother from camp: "I don't have enough
scrunchies! Everybody here has like thirty scrunchies!"
Her mother sends a box of scrunchies
made from quilting scraps & old bra straps.
She wants to die. She draws a *Guess?* label
onto the butt of some jeans from Sears.
The fifth-grade student body disapproves.
She gets back on the horse; she asks a boy to dance.
The boy says, "With a dog?" His lacrosse buddies
erupt in a chorus of barking & belching.
She buys a T-shirt so she has something to cry into.
She steals a pair of shoes so she can get away faster.
When her stepfather picks up the phone, she says,
"I'm going to jail." She sings Mozart's "Lacrimosa"
in the back of the cruiser. She holds a Mr. Coffee
carafe against her inner thigh. The Cure's
Pornography plays on & on. Her prom date
comes drunk in a Mickey Mouse tux.
They dine & dash. He goes down on her
with a Maglite flashlight. "This is the labia
majora," he says with a poke. "This is the labia
minora," he says with a poke.
She flunks out of community college because
slam poetry is more important. She drops out
of slam poetry because, "Swing dancing!"
She brings a man home. "Wait here," she breathes.
She puts on a crinoline, a 1950s prom dress,
coral lipstick & a dead woman's stockings.
She runs back into the man's arms:
"Oh, Dennis! Don't take me behind the bleachers!
I'm a virgin! I have to be home by eleven!"
The man blinks at her. She doubles down,
rips her bodice, slaps herself, says:
"How dare you, Dennis! I'm the prom queen!"

The man leaves. She tries to sleep her way
through the zodiac. She offers a defense
in her journal: "For all *intensive* purposes,"
she writes, "I'm doing it for my art."
She takes a swig from a beer with three butts in it.
She orders the shrimp scampi
and feels real sophisticated.
A man says, "What do you really want?"
She says, "To be the most important poet
of my generation." The man looks away.
"I feel sorry for you," he says.
"I think you're going to lead a very lonely life."
In the bay, a man-of-war brushes against her arm
like the tall, preoccupied stranger at a party
where her wine is about to leave three long welts
on the arm of the hosts' white leather couch.

TENNESSEE WEDDING ON VHS

Here I come down the aisle again, all ablush
and halting across the carpet's carnation plush.

The man at the altar unblinking—eyes negative
black—his smile striving forth to get me, guts me,
                    stops me lockstep.

His smile down under the hem of my frothy things,
fingering the bones of my catfish corset
                    like he can guess my true name.

A tail tumbles out the back of his morning coat.
        A splice.
He turns to the pastor, says,
"Someone's been telling lies about us."

I'm kneeling at the altar. The pastor calls for
                    the laying on of hands:
"Who will bless this woman's tender heart and loins?"
        A silence.

Not the groomsmen. They are newspaper flat.
The bridesmaids have long since dissolved
like sugar in their satin shoes.
                    This is how "I do."

        A shake.
There's our waxed limo lurching forth.
There's his slaw-white boutonniere
        against the green hills of Tennessee.

        A scratch.
Then I am perched on his mother's vinyl ottoman.
        She props her embolismic ankles on my lap.
        She sees babies under my peplum hips.

Cottonmouths slink through the French doors,
    coil round my kitten heels.
The men on the porch take turns handling
    my husband's ten-foot fishing pole.

    A prayer.
"He will crush your head, and you will strike his heel."
    Everyone's drunk on milk punch.
    No one's watching where they step.

During the Super Bowl spectacular,
    a stray pig gets loose on the field.
    A cheer goes up.
Something tickles my insides like a catfish whisker.

Quietly, my father-in-law feeds me
    frosting roses from his finger.
From the kitchen, we hear,
    "I'll get a gun in her hand if it kills her."

HIT IT

You don't have to believe in the Devil
to end up with him. God's not so easy.

Say God takes the form of an egret.
Say the Devil also takes the form of an egret.

Both have a habit
of standing all spooky on the East Texas streets.

They wait sober and ghostly
for your car in the night.

And when you come half-drunk round the bend
God-Egret steps calmly aside.

Devil-Egret lets you hit him.

Look, if I have a habit of dressing up
it's because I'm hoping when I do run into the Devil
he might go a little easier on me.

Even the Devil must go gentle around the edges
of my blue polka-dot dress.

Drinking mezcal at Under the Volcano,
a very drunk Russel keeps poking me:

"Every man loves to poke a dot," he says.
Whether you believe in the Devil or not,
is he not a man?

"Men like red," says my manicurist. It's true.
Red fingernails still slay them like it's 1942.

On the vibrating pleather throne, I submit.
A doll-sized fan dries the wet red tips of each hand.

"Dear God, my head," I say. The fumes are bad.
And now she's gone to work on my feet.

Some facts about the Devil:

He likes to hide in your glove compartment.
He's a yellow bug light in your basement.
When you can see your heartbeat in your fingertips,
or your skirt gets too tight in the waist, He's close.

And now a coat of Quik-Dry.
Don't breathe:

as you careen home from the bar,
as your phone begins its lap dance,
as you come to the crossroads in the moonlight

and the egret that appears there, stays there.
What choice do you have? Say the Devil-Egret
is the only egret. Then hit it.

THE AFTERLIFE OF MY LOST BLAZERS

And then the Devil will bring me to a basement
where we will be reunited: me and my blazers.
Hundreds upon hundreds of them, on hangers,
or hillocks I must eternally rifle through:
the blind worms inching down the wales
of the corduroy, my soul turning out
all the pockets. I must piece this together:
this project the worms must undo, pressing
their wet mouths into elbow patches, under-
mining the plaid and mothing the wool.
My soul tries to try on the jean jackets.
The shoulders don't fit because I have
no shoulders. Is this the Hell of being
immaterial on a mountain of material?
In life I mourned the loss of my blazers,
left on the backs of chairs, in the backs of taxis.
In the afterlife they fall right through me.
Sometimes little things fall out: knotted
cherry stems, cough-drop wrappers, eighty-three
cents, a gas receipt, and once, a matchbook
with something scribbled inside: "Karyna,
you wasted so much of my time. *Burn this*."

ACKNOWLEDGMENTS

Many thanks to the hardworking editors of the following journals where many of the poems in this book first appeared, sometimes in earlier forms.

The Academy of American Poets' *Poem-a-Day*, *AGNI*, *Bat City Review*, *Black Warrior Review*, *Columbia Poetry Review*, *Court Green*, *Drunken Boat*, *Fifth Wednesday*, *Fogged Clarity*, *GlitterPony*, *Horsethief*, *Kenyon Review*, *Lungfull*, *Memorious*, *Ninth Letter*, *Pebble Lake Review*, *Phantom Limb*, *Phoebe*, *Quarterly West*, *Queen of Cups*, *The Rumpus*, *Salt Hill*, *Sixth Finch*, *Southwest Review*, *Spork*, *Stirring*, *Subtropics*, *The Literary Review*, *Verse Daily*, *West Branch*, and *Witness*.

"Elegiac Stanzas (with Rhinestones)" was included in *Not Somewhere Else But Here: A Contemporary Anthology of Women and Place* (Sundress Publications, 2014). "When Someone Says I Love You," "Ouvrir," and "You Are My New God" were included in *Read Women: An Anthology* (Locked Horn Press, 2014).

I am grateful to the many generous and talented folks who've inspired, supported, and gotten down in the weeds with me during this process.

Thank you to the Wisconsin Institute for Creative Writing and to my Madison friends and fellows: Sean Bishop, Bri Cavallaro, Adam Fell, PR Griffis, Jordan Jacks, Amaud Jamaul Johnson, Josh Kalscheur, Jesse Lee Kercheval, Mika Taylor, and Ron Wallace.

Thank you to the University of Houston Creative Writing Program, *Gulf Coast*, Inprint, Poison Pen Reading Series, and the crew at Black Hole Coffee.

Shout-outs to my Houston mafia: Conor Bracken, Audrey Colombe, Katie Condon, Josh Urban Davis, Tony Hoagland, Josh Gottlieb-Miller, Janine Joseph, J. Kastely, Jameelah Lang, Brooke Lightfoot,

Beth Lyons, Sam Mansfield, Zachary Martin, David Tomas Martinez, Misty Matin, Patricia McMahon, Michelle Oakes, Bryan Owens, Nancy Pearson, Justine Post, Kevin Prufer, Martin Rock, Michael Snediker, Analicia Sotelo, Russel Swensen, Becca Wadlinger, Dane Wisher, and Michael & Nina Zilkha. Thank you!

Many thanks to Linda Gregerson, Rebecca Hazelton, Ada Limón, Adrian Matejka, Ray McDaniel, Erika Meitner, Carly Joy Miller, Wayne Miller, Beau Paul, Zachary Schomburg, Diane Seuss, and Erin Elizabeth Smith.

To my colleagues and students at Oberlin College.

To Frederic Gable for the use of his stunning cover photo: *merci beaucoup!*

To the Sarabandistas for their hard work and continued support.

To my family and my partner with love and awe. Mom, Bob, Zoe, Anna, Molly, Kristen, Brent: I feel so lucky to share a life with y'all.

And, finally, to my best friend/writing buddy, Adam Theriault: "Thank you" doesn't even cover it. I owe you *all* the prosecco & grapefruit!

KARYNA MCGLYNN is the author of *I Have to Go Back to 1994 and Kill a Girl* (Sarabande Books, 2009) and three chapbooks. Her poems have recently appeared in *The Kenyon Review*, *Ploughshares*, *Black Warrior Review*, *AGNI*, *Ninth Letter*, *Witness*, and The Academy of American Poet's *Poem-A-Day*. Karyna holds an MFA in Poetry from the University of Michigan, and earned her PhD in Literature and Creative Writing from the University of Houston where she served as poetry editor and managing editor for *Gulf Coast*. Her honors include the Verlaine Prize, the Kathryn A. Morton Prize, the Hopwood Award, and the Diane Middlebrook Fellowship in Poetry at the University of Wisconsin. She is currently a Visiting Assistant Professor of Poetry and Translation at Oberlin College. Find her online at www.karynamcglynn.com.

SARABANDE BOOKS is a nonprofit literary press located in Louisville, KY, and Brooklyn, NY. Founded in 1994 to champion poetry, short fiction, and essay, we are committed to creating lasting editions that honor exceptional writing. For more information, please visit sarabandebooks.org.